I0798735

Can They Fix It?

LEVEL 3

/x/

DECODABLES BY jump!

Teaching Tips

Yellow Level 3

This book focuses on the phoneme **/x/**.

Before Reading

- Discuss the title. Ask readers what they think the book will be about.
- Sound out the words on page 3 together.

Read the Book

- Ask readers to use a finger to follow along with each word as it is read.
- Encourage readers to break down unfamiliar words into units of sound. Then, ask them to string the sounds together to create the words.
- Urge readers to point out when the focused phonics phoneme appears in the text.

After Reading

- Encourage children to reread the book independently or with a friend.
- Ask simple questions about the text to check for understanding. Have them find the pages that have the answers to your questions.

North American adaptations © 2024 Jump!
5357 Penn Avenue South
Minneapolis, MN 55419
www.jumplibrary.com

Library of Congress Cataloging-in-Publication Data is available at www.loc.gov or upon request from the publisher.

ISBN: 979-8-88996-798-9 (hardcover)
ISBN: 979-8-88996-799-6 (paperback)
ISBN: 979-8-88996-800-9 (ebook)

Photo Credits

Images are courtesy of Shutterstock.com. With thanks to Getty Images, Thinkstock Photo and iStockphoto. Cover – Francisco Martinez Saez. 4–5 – Stock Holm, Dragon Images. 6–7 – ALIAKSANDR PALCHEUSKI, Menno Schaefer. 8–9 – donatas1205, Roman Samborskyi. 10–11 – Andrius Kaziliunas, Roman Chazov. 14–15 – Shutterstock.

Can you find these words in the book?

box

fix

fox

tux

Can Sam fix the tux? It is a bad fit.

This is Sam. He can fix the tux.

Can Meg fix the fox cub? It is sick.

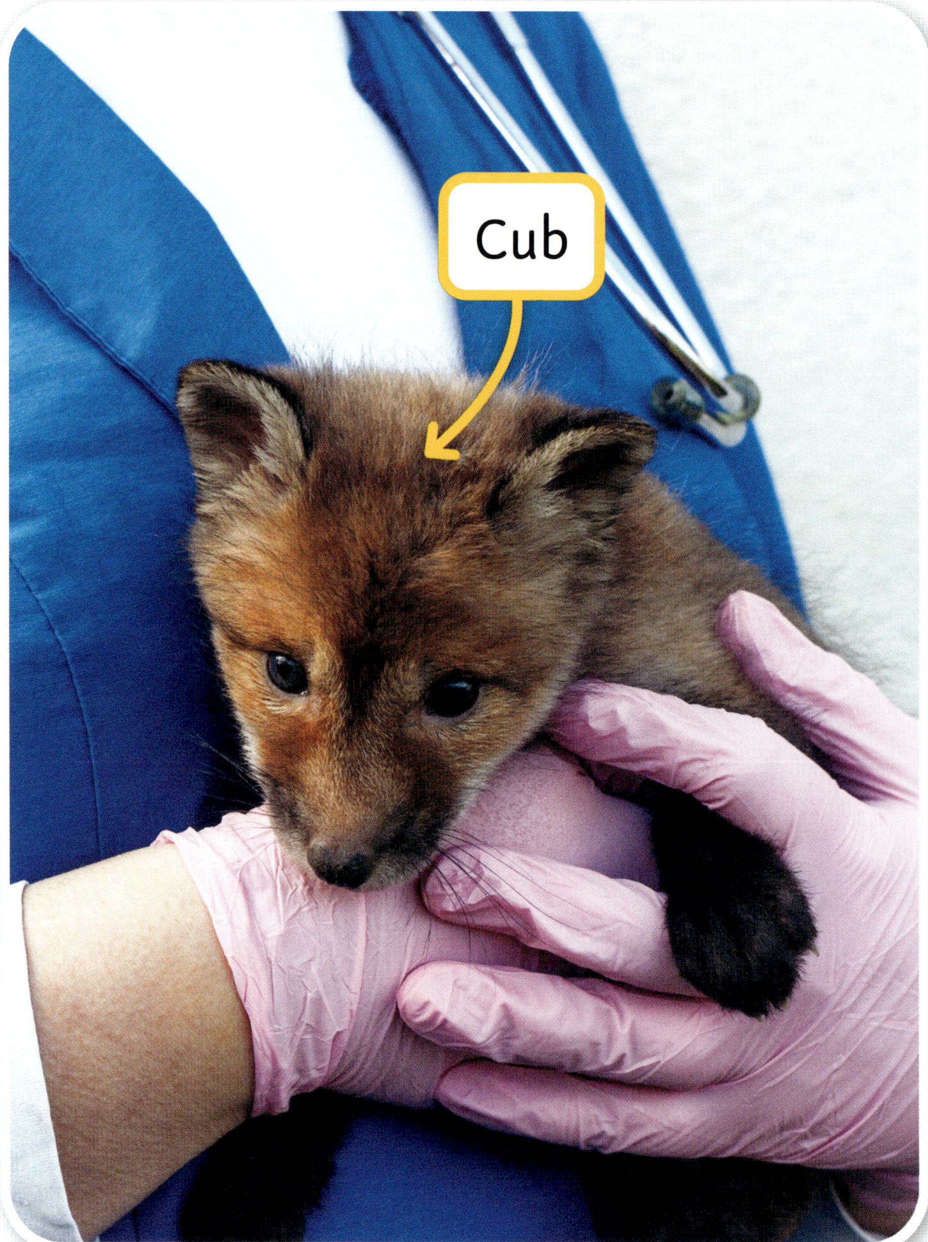

Meg can fix the fox cub.

Can Dex fix the box? The lid is not on.

Dex can fix the box. It has a lid.

Can Kat fix the bus? Pop! Hiss!

Kat can fix the bus.

Can you say this sound and draw it with your finger?

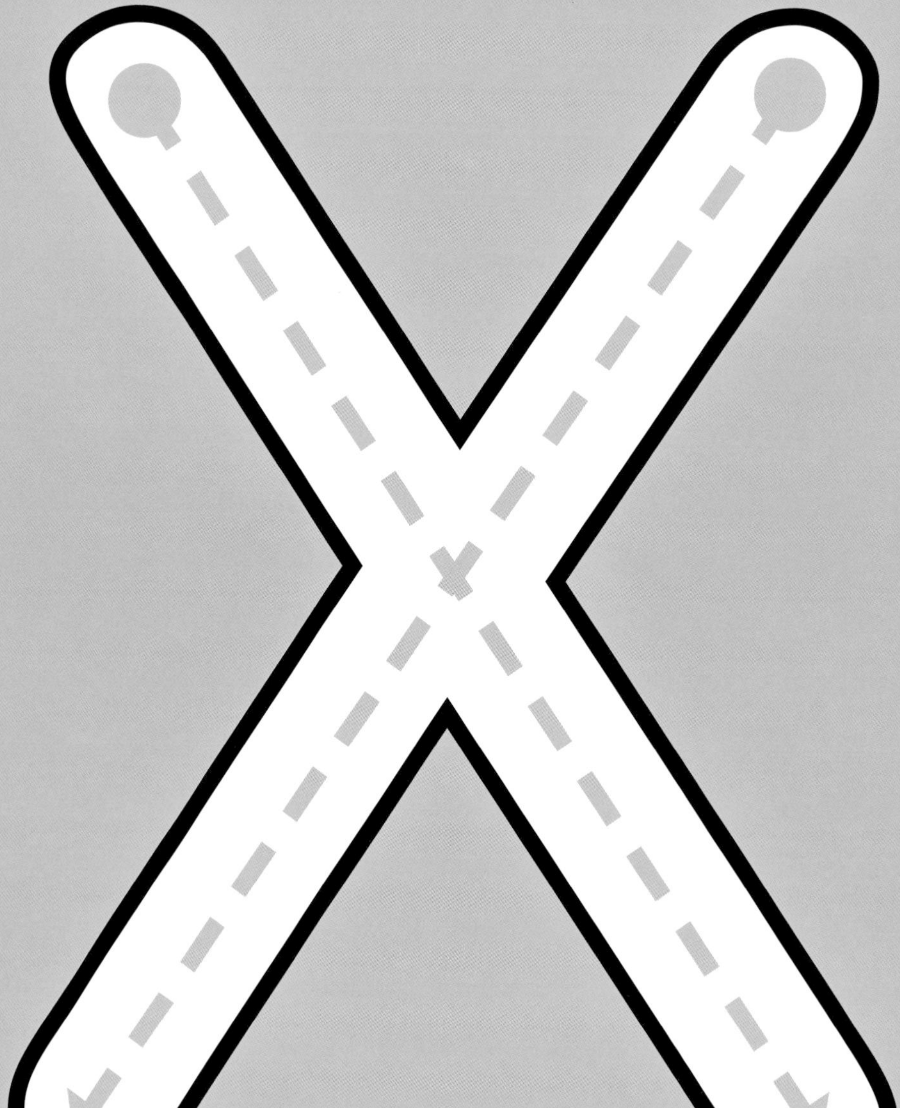

Trace the letter /x/ to complete each word. Say the words out loud.

box

fix

fox

What other words can you spell with /x/?

o__

mi__

wa__

a__e

si__

rela__

Practice reading the book again:

Can Sam fix the tux? It is a bad fit.

This is Sam. He can fix the tux.

Can Meg fix the fox cub? It is sick.

Meg can fix the fox cub.

Can Dex fix the box? The lid is not on.

Dex can fix the box. It has a lid.

Can Kat fix the bus? Pop! Hiss!

Kat can fix the bus.